Finding Your Voice through Creativity

The Art & Journaling Workbook for Disordered Eating

Mindy Jacobson-Levy
&
Maureen Foy-Tornay

gürze books

Finding Your Voice through Creativity
The Art and Journaling Workbook for Disordered Eating

© 2010 by Mindy Jacobson-Levy and Maureen Foy-Tornay

Gürze Books
P.O. Box 2238
Carlsbad, CA 92018
760-434-7533
bulimia.com

Cover design by Rob Johnson, toprotype.com

ISBN-13: 978-0-936077-30-7
ISBN-10: 0-936077-30-1

NOTE:
The author and publisher of this book intend for this publication to
provide accurate information. It is sold with the understanding that it
is meant to complement, not substitute for, professional medical and/or
psychological services.

3 4 5 9 0 8 6 4 2

Paul, Stephanie, and Colin

&

Ian, Sophia, and Paul

…All our love

TABLE OF CONTENTS

INTRODUCTION

As board certified, registered art psychotherapists who have specialized in the treatment of eating disorders for more than forty collective years, we know that art is a highly effective tool for psychological growth. Making art encourages self-expression and heightens the awareness of thoughts and feelings, both past and present. It is a remarkable tool for recovering our right to be heard, letting go of perfectionism, and restoring self-acceptance. And it can foster self-discovery by opening new, symbolic doors into our hearts and minds. Creativity connects us to our "inner voice;" healing occurs when we listen!

Art also bypasses the flow of thoughts and words that continually run through our heads. Although words can be meaningful and lead to healthy action if they're connected to our internal life, they can also serve as a façade that masks true feelings. This is particularly true for individuals with chaotic eating patterns whose negative self-talk has become a habit and focal point.

So we decided to create a "journal" in which words became the backdrop for another form of expression—the creation of art. Our intention was that the pages of the book would literally serve as a canvas for thoughts and feelings "spoken" primarily through images, and then elaborated upon through structured writing. No such workbook addressing disordered eating through these two modalities existed, so the need was certainly there!

Is this book for you?

This is a creative workbook for anyone who wants to explore their relationship with food and their bodies in a new way. Maybe you're already in treatment for an eating disorder, are thinking about entering therapy, or just want a little help getting to know yourself and your needs. Perhaps you're not satisfied with the way you eat, the way you look, or the way you think about food and your body. You might be wondering if you even *have* a problem and whether your particular thoughts and behaviors around food are healthy or normal. However it came to be in your hands, *if you're interested in connecting to your inner voice and listening to what it has to say, then this book is for you.*

The primary intention of this workbook is to assist you in sorting out why you do what you do, and how you might do things differently. It offers many opportunities to experiment with another way of "talking," by using color, lines, shapes, collage, photographs, and drawing. Our hope is that you have fun in the process, trusting that art is a healthy healing tool.

We encourage you to work directly on the pages of the book by taking a chance on the understanding that you can't "mess up." Whatever you draw or write is absolutely acceptable and "good enough." This might feel out of character and drive the perfectionist side of you a bit crazy, but self-discovery is about taking risks!

This journey entails making art and journaling about what you've created. Some of the tasks will help you visualize positive ways to manage stress and develop better ways to assert your needs. Others will make clearer the origin of your struggles with food and body image and the reasons why you continue to embrace unhealthy coping patterns. All will use the creative process to lead you inward to discover what your inner voice has to say.

The drawings and images you make with various art materials will become your *personal signature*, which help you identify and own your feelings. The tools for recovery and growth are present in your art. Accessing them is another story, which is why we wrote this book!

A Note to Readers

The goal of this book is not to teach you about eating disorders or figure out if you indeed have one. We are not challenging you to self-diagnose, nor are we suggesting that this book is a substitute for treatment. Eating disorders are serious illnesses with life-threatening, medical consequences, so if you think you might have an eating disorder please seek professional help.

Nor is this workbook intended to be a substitute for art psychotherapy treatment. However, working in conjunction with an art psychotherapist will enhance its use, as they are professionally trained to explore the manifest/latent content of art renderings and use the creative process for psychological growth and insight.

How to use this workbook

The workbook is organized into chapters that address a variety of topics related to disordered eating and body image disturbance. Each chapter builds on the one that precedes it and is a foundation for the next. For this reason, we recommend that you start at the beginning of the book and work your way through the chapters in order.

Following each drawing task are structured writing exercises. We suggest that you complete each drawing before peeking at the corresponding journal question, since this might influence what you decide to draw! We also suggest you complete your journal entries in pencil. This will prevent your writing from showing through the paper and interfering with the artwork on the other side. However, these are all just ideas, of course, since you are the "boss" of your workbook!

Creativity is the hallmark of this book, and as such it can be used in a variety of settings: on your own, with a therapist, or even in a group setting.

If you work on the art tasks and journal entries on your own, the book can become a private space to express your innermost feelings and thoughts. Carry it with you, taking advantage of whatever materials are available, or plan special times to work on specific tasks. Hopefully you'll begin to use the book as an alternative to disordered eating behavior or negative self-thoughts. This book can also complement or augment therapy that you're already doing. In this case, you might work on tasks on your own and then share them with your therapist. Together, you might then talk about your artwork and journal entries, using them as a springboard for deeper self-awareness and psychological growth, or to jumpstart things when a stalemate is occurring.

When used in a self-help group with peers or within a therapy group setting, each individual might work on his/her own drawing and journal entry, which would then be discussed by group at large. Whether the group is self-run or therapist led, the goals would include self-discovery through group sharing and disclosure.

Questions to Ask When Looking at Your Artwork

There are many lessons to be learned from your works of art. Here are some questions to get you started, which we hope will spark others.

- What do I first notice when I look at the art I just made? What specific words come to mind?

- If I continue to look at my artwork, what else do I notice?

- Is there a focal point in the drawing?

- What do I notice about the line quality? Does it reflect particular feelings?

- What do I notice about the colors I used? Do they reflect a mood or feeling state?

- How much of the page space did I use, and how does that affect how I see my artwork?

- How do I feel when I look at my art?

- Does the picture seem harmonious or discordant (jarring)?

- If I were to "jump into the picture," would my feelings about the art piece change? If so, how?

- What words come to mind when I look at my artwork?

- What would I title my artwork?

A Note to Professionals

This workbook provides structured art tasks and journal prompts related to many aspects of recovery from disordered eating. Each chapter's introduction describes the focus of the tasks that follow, serving as a guide. Your clients may complete a task independently and share it with you in session, or you may have them work on tasks that parallel the therapy work in progress.

Most importantly, we anticipate that this workbook will provide your client with a creative vehicle to "self-express and self-soothe." Again, this is not a step-by-step, therapist-driven, recovery workbook. The client is in the driver's seat, hopefully taking risks of his/her own choosing.

Art Supply Suggestions

You certainly don't need an art studio to be creative! The list that follows contains ideas for basic supplies that will inspire your creativity when you're ready to work. You will see that we have not chosen to include many wonderful art materials, such as oil pastels or watercolors, as we have concerns about their compatibility with the paper (e.g. may soak through the page, smear, etc.). If you can't find specific supplies locally, we have included a list of online art resources on page 153.

Basic Supply List:

Drawing Pencil

Eraser

Pocket pencil sharpener

Pen

Ruler

Crayons

Scissors

Glue

Magazines and newspapers
  [for collage images – words & pictures]

Additional Supplies For Consideration:

Colored markers – fine/broad tip
  [non-permanent]

Colored pencils

Gel pens in a rainbow of colors

Chalk Pastels

Super Hold Hairspray
  [prevents chalk pastels from smearing]

Tempera block paints & brushes

CHAPTER 1

Let's Be Selfish for a Minute

This chapter is about you. How often do you take the time to think about yourself?

The world is a busy place, with lots of external distractions occurring at an extremely fast pace. It's easy to understand how you might get sidetracked by the events, obligations, and people in your life. Perhaps all these things cause you to overlook yourself and your needs in the process of living each day. How many of the statements below relate to you?

- I get so busy with all the things I have to do that I forget to eat during the day.

- I don't have time to make meals, so I consume handfuls of whatever is around instead of healthy options.

- I get wrapped up in my relationships and spend much of my free time on the phone and the computer.

- I have so many responsibilities that I don't have time to rest, relax, or take care of myself.

- I rarely get enough sleep and often feel exhausted.

- Exercise is an all-or-nothing thing for me; it never feels balanced or pleasurable.

- I'm hard on myself.

If this sounds like you: Do you ever wonder how your life got so jam-packed? What do you think would happen if you consciously decided to spend more time on *you*?

In this chapter, we are officially giving you permission to put yourself first, in the limelight, on your own personal stage. Eating patterns that are chaotic and unhealthy may indicate that you feel unheard or misunderstood in another area of your life that has nothing to do with food. Giving yourself the opportunity to *listen within* may help you figure out what might be driving your disordered eating. It may also help you feel more alive, engaged in your life, and happier.

If you don't like the idea of being "selfish," try thinking about this word in a new way. Often people with disordered eating patterns do not pay *enough* attention to themselves because they are so focused on other people's needs. But you will not be neglecting anyone's needs by focusing on your own. On the contrary! When you are feeling nurtured and understood at a deep level, you will have much more to offer other people. Plus, you will have gained self-knowledge, inner strength, and a storehouse of compassion in the process. It's a win-win situation!

So, this is the time and place to explore and reflect on your perceptions of your life and your world. You will start by acknowledging your name, decorating it, and writing about that experience. Then you'll embellish a friend's name and explore the differences between how you treat yourself in comparison. This is an impor-

tant concept, because individuals with disordered eating can sometimes forget to take care of themselves even as they nurture others.

Moving forward, you'll explore a bit about yourself through collage-making and then note your observations. You'll also discover your wishes and hopes for the future in the art experience that follows, and the chapter will end with the creation of a time line of significant events in your life.

Self-exploration through art and journaling may be a new experience for you, but we promise you won't regret it. Let's get started...

What Are the Questions You Want Answered?

Let's begin by making a list of at least six questions you would like answered concerning your eating patterns, the way you view your body, the way you feel "in" your body, how you feel about yourself, or other issues in your life. Here are a few examples:

• Why do I become anxious around certain foods?

• Why do I feel self-conscious around other people?

• Why can't I say no to my friends?

1.

2.

3.

4.

5.

6.

Journal Entry

Are you surprised by the questions you asked? Do they shed any light on how comfortable or uncomfortable you feel about yourself and your life?

The Pie of Your Life

Using a pen or pencil, divide the circle, or "pie," into wedges to show how you spend your time, such as at school, at work, daydreaming, obsessing, exercising, watching television, eating, sleeping, doing hobbies or homework, socializing, taking care of others, etc. Make the wedges bigger for things you spend more time doing and smaller for things you spend less time doing. Then, write the name of each activity in the wedge of the appropriate size and decorate it with designs using lines, shapes, dots, and colors to show how that particular activity makes you feel.

CONGRATULATIONS, YOU HAVE JUST DONE YOUR FIRST DRAWING!

Journal Entry

What do you notice about your pie drawing and how you spend your time? Any surprises here? Are you more clear about why you have been "drawn to" this workbook?

Decorating Your Name

Write your name in whatever way you wish, and then decorate it. Use lines, colors, or shapes to doodle or draw specific things. Have fun!

Journal Entry

What do you notice about how you wrote your name? Is it big or small, spread out or contained? How about the colors? Is it colorful or black-and-white? Do you have any observations about your drawing and how it might reflect something about you?

Your Name Is Your Best Friend

Imagine that your best friend, whom you love and cherish, happens to have the same name as you. Write *their* name below and decorate it, keeping them in mind while you do it.

Journal Entry

How did that feel? Even though both you and your friend have the same name, do you notice any differences between the ways you decorated them? For example, is there a difference in your use of color, brightness, size, or line quality? Does this say anything about how you feel about yourself vs. others?

5   *"This Is Me" Collage*

Look through some magazines and newspapers and find words and pictures that say something about YOU. Cut out whatever catches your eye that you can "relate to" and glue it down on the page. Don't think too hard! You don't have to figure out *why* you chose the words or pictures or what they might mean. We have plenty of time for that!

Journal Entry

Take a look at your collage and jot down any thoughts you might have about it. How did you feel making it? Did you have fun? Are you aware that you have that creative energy inside you, waiting to emerge? See, art is expressive and it can be enjoyable!

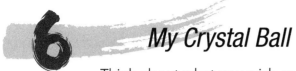

My Crystal Ball

Think about what you wish and hope for, and fill in the sentence below.

"I wish, I hope, I want _____."

Now draw a crystal ball, and create a picture inside that reflects your hopes and dreams.

Journal Entry

How much confidence do you have that you'll achieve your hopes and dreams?

_____My dreams will NEVER come true

_____My dreams MIGHT come true

_____My dreams will SURELY come true

Why do you think you checked off the sentence that you did?

Life Events Time Line

Create a time line of your life. Start by drawing a line—straight, curvy, or angular—from the left side of the page to the right. Then, divide the line by marking every five years of your life, up to your current age.

Now, think about the significant events that affected you during each five-year period and write them down above or below the line. These might include achievements, special events, relationships, changes, losses, puberty, body image issues, positive and negative memories involving food etc. You may choose to personalize your time line with small collage pictures or drawings.

7 *Journal Entry*

Have you ever shared your life story with another person? How do you feel when you talk about yourself with others? Is there someone with whom you'd like to share your time line? Try journaling about some or all of these questions.

CHAPTER 2

Opening Your Heart

In the last chapter you had the opportunity to think about yourself, rather than focusing on anyone or anything else. Perhaps you discovered something new about how you see yourself in comparison to others, or maybe a light bulb went on after you completed your life events time line. Were you surprised by some of the experiences you have had in your life? Do you see a relationship between anything from your past and your current views and feelings about yourself?

In this chapter we encourage you to continue investigating your inner world by taking an even closer look at your emotional life. Imagine what you might find given the opportunity to "walk through your heart" and learn more about how you view yourself, including thoughts and feelings related to:

- intelligence
- sense of humor
- attractiveness and body image
- self-acceptance
- self-esteem
- belonging
- emotions or moods

Think of it like sorting through a closet full of "emotional stuff." While you treasure some of the memories and feelings from your particular life history, others might be upsetting and leave you feeling bad about yourself. In the past, this negative self-view may have pushed you to abuse food and other behaviors even though doing so is an ineffective, short-term solution. Now, though, is a chance to embrace and express *all* the thoughts and feelings inside, not only those that are pleasant, but also those that are uncomfortable.

Note that the corresponding journal entries in this chapter will likely open your eyes to a new way of thinking about your drawings and self, and you'll begin to speak what we call the "feeling language" of art. What this means is that creating art, even when you're not an artist, can help you begin to put feelings into words, especially when you aren't sure exactly what the words are. In this way, art is actually a language in that it makes it easier for you to "speak from the heart."

Here, you will speak from the heart in a number of creative ways. You'll learn how to translate the events in your life into colors, lines, and shapes that represent your deeper emotions. Then you'll create a self-portrait using these forms, which is an inventive way to see yourself! You'll also construct a door to the inner self that will illustrate not only what you allow others to know about you, but also what you might keep hidden.

Some of the art and journal experiences will be abstract, and in others you will be offered a chance to represent your life in familiar forms.

This may include pictures and words from magazines (collage), or using flowers and plant images to represent your life. Using images and words together in a symbolic way will help you gain insight about yourself, while having fun at the same time.

This means it's time for you to grab your microscope, take a risk, and look at yourself and your life in greater detail. Are you ready to open *your* heart?

Decoding Your Life Events Time Line

Review the life events time line from Chapter One (p. 25) and on this page, translate it into color, lines, and shapes. Starting on the left side of the page with the 0-5 year category, make a vertical strip of colors/lines/shapes for that age range, then continue in the same fashion for the 5-10 year category, 10-15 year category, etc. Imagine how the themes in each age group might be interpreted using color and design.

8 *Journal Entry*

What do you notice about the feeling tone throughout your "abstractly-decorated" time line? Are you aware of any connections between the events noted in each category and shifts in mood, as reflected by color/line/shape? Do you have any recollections about specific issues, such as your self-esteem, body image, relationship with food, or feelings of safety or competency during any of the five-year time periods?

Abstract Self-Portrait

It's time to experiment with seeing yourself in a new light. Using lines, colors, and shapes, create an abstract self-portrait. There should be nothing that looks realistic here, nothing that one might identify as a human form—just shapes and colors that say something about you. RELAX, put on some music, chill out a little, and make art about "YOU."

Journal Entry

How did you like doing this task? Was it entertaining or anxiety producing? Do you get concerned when things aren't clear and recognizable, as in this abstract task? What is the tone or mood of your self-portrait? For instance, is it bold, quiet, organized, scattered, expansive, contained, or some other quality? Are you able to identify any parallels between your abstract self-portrait and how you actually "see" yourself on an emotional level?

Abstract Self-Image Translation

Now that you've experimented with abstract forms, try to translate them into words and images. Using newspapers and magazines, find pictures and words that you believe match up with specific areas of your abstract self-image. If one portion of your picture has a large purple circle, see if you can find a picture or words that make you think of the purple circle. Remember, there is no such thing as "right," "wrong," "good," or "bad" in this workbook. Sometimes you learn a great deal when you just wing it!

10 *Journal Entry*

Thoughts? Did you learn anything new about yourself after translating your abstract self-image into representational forms and words? Are there any connections between the journal entry from the abstract self-portrait (p. 31), or the images and the journal entry from the "This Is Me Collage" (p. 21)? Have any hidden themes emerged?

The Door to the Inner Self

Create a door to represent the entrance to your inner self, where your feelings "live." Consider details such as: what materials the door would be made of (e.g. wood, metal or bamboo), whether it has windows, peepholes, or locks, and what color(s) it might be. Add whatever you believe is important until it feels complete.

Journal Entry

What do you notice about the door? What would it convey to other people who might approach? Is it welcoming, uncertain, or is the message *stay away*? Are any mixed messages apparent?

My Secret Garden

In the last task you created a door to represent an entrance into your inner sanctuary. Imagine a garden inside, which reflects your feelings or emotions. The garden might be comprised of an assortment of flowers, plants, vegetables, fruits, and weeds. It might also include a sitting area, birdfeeders, or other objects. Draw what your garden would look like.

12 *Journal Entry*

Describe your garden, including how it looks. Is it flourishing and carefully tended, or is it in need of a gardener? In this chapter, the goal was for you to take a few steps inward. Does your inner garden tell you any "secrets" about the degree of balance and stability you have in your life?

CHAPTER 3

Emotional Armor

Armor is a type of body covering that is worn for protection. Animals have natural forms of armor such as shells, horns, claws, teeth, and scents that guard them from harm. Humans engage in various jobs and sports that require protective outerwear as well. Football players don helmets and pads to prevent injury, nurses wear gloves for safety, law enforcement officers carry weapons for self-defense, and ballerinas wear toe shoes to protect their feet as they twirl across the hardwood floor. In your various roles in life, you may wear armor, too.

In this chapter we'd like to introduce the concept of "emotional armor," which is also a form of protection, but different than physical armor in that it is usually hidden. Think of it as an invisible shield that you put up in response to situations between you and other people so as not to reveal your true feelings.

Emotional upsets often unintentionally prompt the creation of this type of protective covering. Some examples are:

- Laughing when you're feeling anxious
- Shutting down when you're angry
- Snapping or shouting at others when your feelings are hurt
- Shifting the focus from yourself to another person when you're embarrassed about something you've said or done
- Withdrawing from others to avoid conflicts

In any given situation, emotional armor can be either helpful or harmful. For example, if you're upset about something personal and don't wish to share it at work or school, emotional armor helps you keep it in a contained, safe place! We all wear emotional armor from time to time, and in most cases it is a helpful tool for healthy living.

But emotional armor can also be destructive, as is the case with eating disorders and other self-harming behaviors. It can suppress spontaneity, censor creativity, and interfere with problem solving. It creates barriers between people, making intimacy difficult because the truth is often denied. In the extreme, a person can become so accustomed to armor that it's like a prison! So even though the rituals of disordered eating *do* offer a form of security, our question to you is, "At what price?" Isn't the weight of emotional armor, including a focus on food intake, calorie or fat gram counting, body image, and exercise, a heavy burden to bear? Is it truly "protection?"

In this chapter, we encourage you to explore the armor that *you* wear when performing your current life roles. For example you might be a student, employee, friend, daughter or son, sister or brother, parent, spouse, or partner. But how you feel about each of those roles may surprise you. Does each one support your wellbeing, or are some antagonistic? Thumbs up or thumbs down?

When asked to describe your armor, will you draw yourself as a super hero, an ancient warrior, or a Greek mythological God? This is your chance to really use your imagination. Writing a daring letter without sending it will give you the freedom to approach concealed feelings without any negative consequences!

Perhaps you've contemplated what your life would be like if you *didn't* use disordered eating as a form of armor. Maybe you're unsure of how to use armor in healthier ways. Fortunately, as you become more self-aware and communicate your inner feelings more openly, the heavy armor you've worn for so long may seem less essential and you'll be ready to take it off.

So, let's take this next step towards recovery by learning about armor and how you might choose to use it safely and effectively!

 *Life Roles*

Identify and make a list of the roles that you engage in on a regular basis, for example, student, friend, daughter, wife, mother, etc. Divide the page into squares that equal the number of roles on your list. Write one job title or role in each square, and decorate the inside with colors/lines that reflect that role. When you're finished draw a "thumbs up" in the corner of the box containing the role that you favor most, and a "thumbs down" in the box containing the role that you favor least.

Journal Entry

Are you surprised by the number of roles you have in your life? Which one do you spend the most time doing, and is that the life role you *most* enjoy? Which role do you spend the least time doing, and is that the life role you *least* enjoy? If you had the opportunity to shift your roles around, which one do you wish you *could* be doing most of the time? What prevents you from doing that?

Draw Yourself in Armor

Find a close up photograph of your face that you're comfortable using for an "armored self" drawing. Cut your head out of the photo and glue it on the page below. Let your imagination go wild: envision your favorite comic book hero, cartoon character, Greek mythological God, or warrior of antiquity. Using this as a starting point, create meaningful armor for yourself. In other words, draw yourself in any kind of gear or garb that you believe you need in order to protect yourself. What would you be wearing or need to have with you to be effective in battle?

Journal Entry

Write a bit about how your armor protects you in your daily life. What kinds of things does it protect you from, and how does it do that? Does your armor restrict you in any way?

 *The Secret Toll of Wearing Armor*

Wearing emotional armor means shielding others, as well as yourself, from your authentic feelings. Those inner feelings remain hidden, and more "acceptable" emotions are conveyed instead. It's time to have a conversation between the "crowd pleaser" you, and the true *self* that you protect with armor. Pick a different colored pencil for each part of you and "chat" in the space below. Just for fun, use both your non-dominant and dominant hands to write. Let the conversation begin!

Journal Entry

What do you notice about the conversation between the "crowd pleaser" you, and the true self that you protect with armor? Are you surprised by anything that was written? What would happen if you let your hidden feelings come to the surface more often?

 *The Letter You Would Never Send*

Do you have thoughts and feelings that you've wanted to communicate to someone, but never had the courage? Perhaps the timing wasn't right, you had concerns about offending them, or you were scared. Here's an opportunity to write a letter that you'd never send—at least for now. Begin by designing a decorative border on the perimeter of the page to represent privacy. Then pick someone with whom you'd like to "talk" and let those feelings flow!

Journal Entry

Take a breath. How did that feel? What was it like getting your feelings out on paper? Can you think of other people to whom you'd like to "talk" through this type of letter writing? Who might they be, and what would you like to say to them?

 **_A Suit of Armor vs. An Umbrella_**

Although armor does serve a protective function, it can sometimes be excessive or extreme. We'd like you to rethink the personal armor you created for yourself in Task 14 (p.43), and consider using the metaphor of a sturdy umbrella instead. This would shield you from harmful external elements, but could easily be closed when no longer needed. Draw and then decorate an umbrella that would serve this purpose for you—protection that you can _use_ when you _choose_.

Journal Entry

What does the umbrella you just created suggest about the type of personal armor you desire? How did you decorate it? How big is it and would it safely shield you from the elements? How do you feel about having the option of controlling your use of personal armor, just like opening and closing an umbrella?

CHAPTER 4

Finding Your Voice

Every day, in a variety of ways, we respond to life. We smile at a puppy rolling in the grass, cry when a best friend moves away, hide from the harsh words of a co-worker. These are all reactions shaped by one's feelings and history of expressing them. We need a way to express ourselves when powerful emotions push forward. It is a way of taking action and communicating to others what is going on with us.

Sometimes, though, we are not ready or able to communicate our emotions. Perhaps they are too strong, their origin isn't apparent, or we don't have the skills to decipher them clearly. If this is the case, our emotions can become stifled and express themselves through physical symptoms. Frustration shows itself through a headache, or fear gets lodged in a belly that feels full or painful.

In the same way, hidden or private feelings can be expressed through symptoms of an eating disorder. Sadness can constrict the heart and take away hunger, while anger can morph into body dissatisfaction and shame. Bingeing and purging, restricting, over-exercising, and abusing laxatives, diet pills, or diuretics are all "warning signs" that your true feelings are barricaded within the body. Can you see how your body "speaks" and that listening inward might reveal a rainbow of emotions begging to be discovered?

In earlier chapters, you have gotten to know yourself a little better by focusing on who you are and what you believe about life and the world. You've also explored some of your hidden emotions by opening your heart and discovered that you might be using your disordered eating as a form of armor or protection. Now, we encourage you to begin the process of "finding your voice" by embracing and owning your feelings and reactions, whatever they may be. Learning how to effectively listen to the voice of your inner self and honor its truth will both reduce the need for excess armor and decrease eating disorder symptoms.

It takes a lot of hard work to qualify your authentic reactions, connect them to feelings, and communicate them. Although these are skills that many of us commonly practice using words, not everyone is comfortable with that! For some of us music, art, dance, poetry, photography, and other creative outlets help us "speak." That's where this book comes in!

You'll begin by picturing yourself as a machine and exploring your unique reactions. Next, you will take a "feelings inventory" and recognize the complexity of your inner life. "Disposing" of the sentiments that plague you will be a fun way to experience some emotional relief, while the creation of a body map indicating where feelings get "stuck" will surprise you. Finally, you'll speak your mind to the disordered-eating Dictator who has been silencing your emotional voice for far too long!

Is it time to reclaim your thoughts and feelings? Are you ready for some eye-opening creative ventures? We hope so. Let your authentic voice be heard!

You Are a Unique Reaction Machine

No matter what happens around you, you respond in one fashion or another. Simply because you are alive, your "on" switch is activated, meaning you're taking in data, processing it, and "spitting out" responses. Whether or not others witness this internal process, it happens quite naturally and automatically.

Now, think about how machines work and imagine that you are one of them. Consider the type of machine that you would be, your dimensions, the materials you'd be made of, and your function. Draw yourself as this machine.

18 *Journal Entry*

What do you notice about the machine you just created? How does it operate from the outside, and what happens inside? Does your machine have feelings and, if so, how do they get expressed? As a human being, how do you process and react to the positive and negative things that are going on in your life? Does your drawing of a "machine-self" reflect anything you didn't know about yourself?

 **19** *The Yucky Feelings Inventory*

Sometimes you may have feelings that are extremely uncomfortable, difficult, and downright "yucky." While you probably don't want to spend too much time visiting those feelings, doing so can be extremely helpful in terms of healing disordered eating patterns. Once you *know* what those yucky feelings are and what they might be about ("the knowing factor"), you can embrace them, address them directly without abusing food, and move on.

Take "The Yucky Feelings Inventory" by circling all the feelings below that you might be experiencing right now, or that you have struggled with in the past.

Exhausted   Intimidated   Abandoned   Over-protected
Lonely   Angry   Suspicious   Fearful
Exhausted   Unwanted   Rejected   Depressed
Sad   Enraged   Confused   Ashamed   Agitated
Obsessed   Hateful
Fragile   Inadequate   Violent   Inferior
Criticized   Disrespected   Embarrassed   Humiliated
Belittled   Resentful   Controlled   Manipulated
Empty   Pressured   Unheard   Ridiculed
Insignificant   Misunderstood   Uncared For
Trapped   Neglected
Guilty   Scared   Invisible   Abused   Unsupported
Powerless   Cheated   Attacked
Untrusting   Unloved   Afraid   Unsafe
Anxious   Frightened   Threatened   Terrified
Discouraged   Helpless   Depressed

Journal Entry

What was it like to read all those *feeling words* that might be harbored deep inside you? How did it feel to own them by circling them on the page? Was it a relief to get those hidden feelings out in the open?

20 Disposing of Your Feelings

There are many ways to dispose of things you don't want. You can toss them in a trash can, put them down the garbage disposal, bring them to a consignment or thrift shop, or give them away. Regardless of the method, the results are the same: you're getting rid of something. What would serve as the best "disposal" for you? Draw that image and then write or draw all the feelings that you'd like to release. Place them inside the disposal you created…and let them go.

20 *Journal Entry*

Why is it easier to dispose of your feelings rather than embrace them? Maybe at some point in your life you learned that there are consequences if you acknowledge, express, or share feelings. Has anyone ever told you that your feelings are bad, stupid, selfish, scary, unwanted, make you a drama queen/king, are exaggerated, unnecessary, and/or need to be disposed of quickly? Perhaps you are ashamed of them, or are fearful of having them?

Journal about what would happen if you didn't get rid of your feelings quickly, but shared them with others instead.

Storing Feelings in Your Body

Using the feelings that you circled in Task 19 (p. 55), identify places in your body where you believe they "take up residence." In other words, assign each uncomfortable feeling you have to a part of your body where it might reside. Write those feelings in the particular body areas of the figure—representing you—below.

Journal Entry

Feelings don't disappear; they're either stored inside, or a way is found to express them. This doesn't necessarily mean they're resolved, but a first step in that direction is listening inward and identifying what's going on within YOU.

Are there any patterns that you notice about the body-emotions template you just completed, any areas that are most heavily populated by uncomfortable feelings? If so, what are they and do you see a connection between those areas and any unhealthy eating patterns? Do you see links between those feelings and negative feelings about your body?

 *Your Disordered-Eating Dictator*

Somehow, in order to protect or take care of yourself on your life journey, you found it necessary to hide your true beliefs (mind) and feelings (heart). Any difficult thoughts or emotions you experienced became secrets lodged within your body, only to be replaced by dissatisfaction with your hips, breasts, stomach, butt, or other body parts. Do you suppose that by focusing on your imperfect body, you sidestepped being embarrassed by or afraid of your feelings?

Here entered the disordered-eating Dictator, a simultaneous solution for so many things! But who is this inner Dictator that promotes feelings of self-loathing, and what would happen if you confronted the Dictator in an old fashioned tug-of-war?

Find three small pictures from a magazine or newspaper to represent your heart, mind, and the Dictator, and glue them on the page. Taking turns with "the microphone" so that all three voices are heard, write what each part would say to the other.

22 *Journal Entry*

What do you notice about the content of the mind-heart-Dictator conversation that just took place? How do you perceive the Dictator's role in your life? Is it healthy? Do you still believe disordered eating and poor body image are your allies?

CHAPTER 5

Are You Hungry?

In the previous chapter, we talked about how buried feelings can sometimes express themselves as physical symptoms or dysfunctional eating behaviors. We also introduced the idea of "finding your voice," one aspect of which is acknowledging and honoring those feelings and communicating them in appropriate ways. In this chapter, we will continue to explore our inner lives by recognizing that *feelings* are connected to *hungers*, and that when we tune in to one, we can fulfill the other.

Usually when we talk about hunger, we are referring to our body's *physical* need for food. We have other physical needs as well, such as for air, water, shelter, warmth, and sleep. Since these are primary and basic to our health and wellbeing, resolving any unhealthy behavioral patterns that interfere with meeting these needs is critical.

Now, let's expand our definition of hunger to include those things we need on the *emotional* level. These might include such longings as:

- Security
- Acceptance
- Understanding
- Friendship
- Intimacy
- Love
- Spirituality
- Creativity
- Mastery

These kinds of wishes, desires, and emotional cravings are as profound and critical to our wellbeing as physical needs. In the same way we can feel "full" when we have eaten a balanced meal, we can feel "full" when our emotional needs are met. The reverse is also true: Ignoring our emotional needs, such as the fact that we might need a hug or time for spiritual pursuits, can make us feel empty—invisible, disconnected, and unfulfilled.

How, then, can we learn to satisfy ourselves at the emotional level? How do we *know* what our needs are and how to meet them?

A good way to start is by understanding that *emotional needs are directly connected to our feelings*. We long for emotional security, and when family and friends love and care for us, we feel safe. We yearn to be accepted by others, and if we aren't, we feel sad. We want to feel confident, and if we can't master a task, we feel anxious. In this way, we can use our *feelings as guides* by tracing them back to their source. We can tune into ourselves and ask, "What am I feeling right now? And what is the hunger that underlies that feeling?"

Asking these questions and listening for the answers is another way to connect with the wisdom of your inner voice. Chances are, if you have problems with chaotic eating patterns and body scrutiny, you don't have much experience with these skills. You may feel distanced not only from your authentic feelings, but also from the physical and emotional hungers connected to them. The more you practice listening inward, though, the more comfortable you will feel tolerating and expressing your feelings and the more capable you will be of getting your needs met—whether they are physical or emotional. This is another key to *finding your voice.*

So, in this chapter, let's find healthy resources for self-fulfillment by imagining and journaling about longings, wishes, and other emotional hunger pangs.

You'll begin by pairing several disordered-eating statements with the feeling phrases they may represent in order to open up a more honest internal dialogue. Next, you'll use cartoons to illustrate what attracts you to these unhealthy behaviors and how you benefit from maintaining them. This will help you realize that damaging behaviors can only temporarily fill the void of painful feelings and unmet needs.

Next, you'll choose between images of kick-boxing or dancing to represent the conflicts or closeness in your current relationships. Knowing how other people affect you, and influence the way you treat yourself, might expose emotional hungers that have been buried for a long time. You'll also examine family roles in greater detail by creating an abstract "family map" to illustrate which members you feel close to and which you feel distant from. This will be followed by a journal entry that details who is/isn't supportive and why this is the case.

Lastly, you'll complete a detailed, personal instruction manual that communicates exactly how you'd like to be cared for by others. This will be helpful when trying to share your needs with them as you get more confident voicing your feelings.

We admit that assessing your hungers isn't easy! Write your self a positive note about your ability to reconnect with them and position it so that you see it every morning. Positive inspiration is a necessary tool in the healing process. Let's take that optimism and explore the best ways to nourish yourself emotionally!

Unscrambling the Word Match

Have you ever observed a caged hamster running on an exercise wheel? Do you think the hamster realizes that it's going nowhere, and that no matter how fast it runs, it's still in the same place? This is similar to what happens when you ruminate about food, your body, and your weight. While you think you're being productive, you're actually filling your head with internal chatter while the scenery remains constant.

Below are sentences that were created by individuals struggling with disordered eating patterns and poor body-image. The left column contains statements related to food and the body, while the right contains feeling-based phrases. How would you pair these up? Draw lines to match them.

Disordered Eating Statements

I am ugly.

I'm full & never feel hungry.

People like me because of my appearance.

I am the biggest person around.

I am hungry.

I feel heavy.

I am too fat to fit in nice clothing.

I am not good enough to be liked.

It's not how you feel, it's how you look.

I love to be alone.

Eating carbohydrates will make me fat.

There is something wrong with my body.

I wish I was skinny.

You are what you eat.

I have big thighs and must purge.

Feeling Phrases

I try hard not to feel any feelings.

I'll never be the person I want to be.

I am scared and afraid.

There is something wrong with me.

I don't like "me."

I am obsessed with superficial things.

I'm not good enough to be liked.

I feel sick.

I'm never going to be perfect.

I hate what I'm doing to myself.

I wish I was happy with myself.

I need to get something out.

I don't fit in with my family or friends.

I worry what others might think of me.

I have a heavy heart.

23 *Journal Entry*

Talking about feelings is a catalyst for opening up a more honest dialogue with yourself, as well as between you and other people, like your family, friends, or therapist. It will help you understand *why* you do something, so you will have the strength to resist that behavior when you have those feelings again. If you're not connected with your feelings, you're more likely to act them out.

When do you tend to focus most on your body and food? Do you act out with food or excessive body focus when you're upset about something? Have you ever said any of the phrases in the "match-up" exercise on the previous page?

What's on the Menu?

In this task we'd like you to draw the "appetizing" things (the pros) about your current food-related behaviors, meaning how they help you cope with your life. These responses are actually tempting "menu items" that may be hard to resist!

In each of the four boxes below, make a cartoon sketch of one benefit you receive from your eating behaviors that relates to the category or life component identified above that box.

Family

Friends & Relationships

School & Work

Self-Esteem

24 *Journal Entry*

Now that you've completed all four sketches, what do you identify as "appetizing" in maintaining your disordered eating patterns? Do you suppose that any of these behaviors might actually be "a recipe for disaster?"

Let's Dance or Should We Kick-Box?

This task will explore how relationships, whether healthy or toxic, influence our emotional and physical health.

Divide the paper in half by drawing a line either horizontally or vertically. Imagine yourself "dancing" with someone significant in your life. Using colors, lines, and shapes, create an abstract drawing which reflects the emotions that might arise during this dance together and express those emotions on one side of the paper. On the other side of the page, imagine you're in a kick-boxing tournament. With whom would you choose to spar? Once again, use colors, lines, and shapes to reflect the feelings that would arise as you faced them head-on in the boxing ring.

25 *Journal Entry*

How did it feel to work on this task? With whom did you imagine dancing, and what is it about that relationship that leaves you feeling positive? With whom did you choose to spar in the boxing ring picture? What is it about that relationship that prompted you to imagine yourself giving them a right hook?

Now, let's look at your artwork from a different angle. Even though you labeled the dancing relationship positive, could some aspect of that connection have contributed to your disordered eating patterns? Even though you considered the boxing relationship toxic, is there anything caring or supportive about the person you chose to box?

Arranging the Dinner Table

Your family may be a wonderful support on your journey, or they might actually contribute to your eating problems. In order to explore your relationship with them, you're going to create an abstract collage.

Begin by cutting shapes out of colored paper and/or patterned cloth to represent each member of your family, including yourself. Create different shapes and use distinct colors or patterns for each person. Include immediate and/or extended family members and pets that play a significant role in your life.

Arrange the shapes in a configuration that reflects your unique relationship with each member. If you feel close to a particular person, place their shape close to yours on the page. Similarly, if you feel disconnected from someone, place them farther away. Complete the task by gluing the shapes onto the page.

26 *Journal Entry*

What do you notice about the family arrangement that you created? Are you surprised about how things turned out? Whom did you identify as your *support team*, and how do they support you? What about the people farthest away from you on the page? Who are they and what do those dynamics reflect? Are any family members blocking others from relating to one another, and is this helpful or harmful? Make a list of changes you believe would improve your relationships with those individuals you included in your family configuration picture.

 *My Unique Instruction Manual*

Every person experiences emotional hungers, one of which is to be respected and heard by others. Here's a chance to provide the people in your life with a mini "Instruction Manual" that communicates exactly how YOU would like to be treated. Think about what you need and fill in the sheet below.

INSTRUCTION MANUAL FOR: _____

On a day-to-day basis, I'd like you to try to:

1.

2.

3.

When you see that I'm upset about something, please try to:

1.

2.

3.

When you say _____ to me,

I feel _____

because _____ .

In the future, when we _____ ,

I'd prefer if you try your best to _____

rather than _____

because _____ .

Other important things I need to tell you: _____

_____

27 *Journal Entry*

In your Instruction Manual, you attempted to help others understand how you would like to be treated. How did it feel to outline the "TLC" (Tender Loving Care) you need? Who will be most inclined to *listen* to what you have to say and *learn* some new behaviors that might improve your relationship? Would reading your Instruction Manual regularly, adding to it as needed, and sharing it with important people in your life help you in your recovery process?

CHAPTER 6

Panning for Gold

Each of us possesses many wonderful attributes. Acknowledging those strengths and positive characteristics is easy when we feel competent, useful, and worthy. But appreciating our good qualities can be tricky when we are caught up in the unpleasant thoughts, feelings, and behaviors of eating problems, or when we are hiding within the protective shell of our armor. In recovery, it is important to take a more realistic view of ourselves by exploring and celebrating what makes us extraordinary and irreplaceable human beings.

How do we do this? The process is akin to panning for gold, much like the early miners did when they sifted through the sand and water of stream bottoms to find treasure. While you may have to do a lot of "personal sifting" to recognize your hidden value, with perseverance amazing things will rise to the surface where they can shine.

There are talents within your grasp that you may not realize are even there! Maybe you haven't had the opportunity to develop them, or perhaps they've taken a back seat to other responsibilities.

Perhaps you are:

- A wonderful singer
- Attentive to others
- An animal's best friend
- A loyal companion
- Insightful when problems arise
- A math whiz
- Good with detailed work
- An awesome belly dancer
- Great with children
- An imaginative writer
- Clever
- A fashion expert
- Really funny

The creative process in this chapter will strengthen your ability to see these positive qualities—your personal inner gold—in spite of any personal "debris" or critical thinking that may have interfered in the past. This self-affirming journey will begin by identifying yourself as a treasure chest containing precious gems just waiting to be discovered.

This will be followed by the opportunity to learn what others cherish about you, which may not only be surprising, but may also strengthen your motivation to love yourself as they do.

Next, you will learn about "reframing" a past situation that you once deemed negative, which will offer important lessons about how vital it is to be flexible when viewing one's self and one's life. This will be illustrated by a colorfully enhanced self-portrait drawn *directly on* a mirror. How restorative this will be, re-creating yourself in a playful way!

Lastly, you will celebrate an accomplishment or personal trait that you feel is outrageously fabulous by creating a trophy in your honor. When you love and respect yourself "as is," self-worth and confidence are natural consequences. Wouldn't it be amazing to be the best at who you *are* rather than putting your effort into who you *are not?*

Our hope is that this self-discovery expedition will help you begin to see yourself in a more positive light. After all, self-love is part of the key to living a full and healthy life. Let's put on our mining gear and get started!

28 *You Are a Treasure*

Draw a treasure chest that represents YOU and decorate it lavishly, keeping in mind that there is wonderful treasure inside. Place stickers on the box, glue glitter or pictures of gems on it, paint it, or do whatever you want to make it look like a "marvelous find." After all, YOU are a marvelous find! Now, cut five 1"x 4" strips of paper and jot one positive self-statement that *doesn't* have to do with your appearance on each one. Tape them to the drawing.

28 *Journal Entry*

You've just sifted for inner gold! What do you think about the riches you uncovered? Are other people aware of the treasure within the box—all the wonderful qualities you possess?

Others Believe You Are a Treasure Too!

Choose a few family members or friends who "know you" who would be willing to help you with this task. Give each one a self-addressed, stamped envelope containing five 1"x 4" strips of paper (as in the previous task). Ask them to write down five qualities that they admire about you that are unrelated to appearance. Have them mail the envelopes, and get ready for a feel good, self-esteem-boosting reality check! Once you receive their "gifts" of paper strips, tape them to the treasure chest you drew on page 77.

 *Journal Entry*

Are there similarities between what you said about yourself and the observations of others? If so, what are they? Any surprises?

Reframing Your Life

Have you ever noticed how some people can turn a negative situation around and see the positive in it? Here's an opportunity to look at your "self" in a new light.

Divide the page in half by drawing a vertical line separating the two sides. On one side, draw yourself in a past situation in which you'd describe yourself as being "difficult." Perhaps you displayed behavior traits that were not exactly pleasant or socially desirable. List those traits underneath the drawing. Now think about how those same qualities might serve you in a positive way, for instance how might they protect you, help you set boundaries, or perform a task in a different situation. Draw a second scenario on the other half of the page, illustrating how the same "undesirable" qualities might be advantageous and valuable.

30 *Journal Entry*

Is it hard for you to shift gears and take another look at a situation while you're in the midst of it? What might help you see things from a different perspective? How do you know when you're locked into seeing something one way, and only one way? Do others give you these cues?

The Mirror Does Lie

Mirrors reflect two things: your physical appearance and your feeling state. But your perception of what the mirror is revealing can't be trusted if you're fixated on your body image and your food intake. Mirrors also "lie" when your internal preoccupation with perfection results in a jaded, negative view of yourself. How many times have you been self-critical, only to hear a loved one's unsolicited positive comments?

For this task we'd like you to spend five minutes looking at the reflection of your face in a small mirror (i.e., a bathroom mirror that frames your face). With oil pastels*, make a contour drawing directly on the mirror, tracing the lines of your face and hair. Using your imagination develop your portrait by adding different colors. When you're finished, take a digital picture, print it out, and paste it on the page below.

*After you complete the corresponding journal task, you can remove the oil pastels from the mirror by using a dry cloth or one with a small amount of vegetable oil on it.

Journal Entry

Look at the amazing drawing you just completed! How did this self-reflection experience feel to you? Is it hard for you to look in a mirror and abandon the critical voice inside? What could you say to yourself that would help you override the judgmental voice and embrace a more self-accepting one?

Being the Best at Who You Are, Not Who You Aren't

How often do you do something that someone else thinks you'd be good at, rather than listening to your heart's desire? Do you ever buy into others' opinions in lieu of your own, believing that they somehow know you better than you know yourself? How would you like a chance to give yourself an award for something *you* believe is a personal strength?

Let's start with a little fun by identifying and drawing a trophy that reflects something *incredibly outrageous* about you. Next, on a more serious note, think of something that you truly believe you do *amazingly well*. Perhaps it's a healthy behavior you display, a skill that is work or hobby related, or a personality trait that has really gotten you places. Imagine what kind of trophy would reflect that asset and draw it, too.

32 *Journal Entry*

Write about the two trophies you created for yourself. How does it feel to acknowledge and honor who you really are, versus what others expect, think, or want of you?

CHAPTER 7

Trying on a Different Hat

Change is part of everyday life. Some changes are easier than others; some seem easy, but have far-reaching consequences. Choosing to put on a different hat, for instance, is a simple thing to do, yet it can profoundly influence the way we look on the outside, as well as the way we feel about ourselves on the inside.

Any time we move from something familiar to unfamiliar, we are experimenting with change. This may feel awkward at first, but invariably offers a new way of looking at things—which can be quite exciting! However, change can also bring with it feelings of anxiety *in anticipation of* a new experience, or fear *in the midst* of that new experience. These emotions are especially common in response to external factors that may be out of our control such as:

- Changes in existing situations, such as a parental divorce or unexpected medical illness
- Physical changes due to maturation
- Adopting a new pet
- Attending a new school or college
- A job layoff or future job interviews

- Social or professional functions that require meeting others for the first time
- Getting engaged or married
- Expecting a baby
- Traveling during severe weather

In order to master this discomfort, coping behaviors may emerge that are rigid and unhealthy. Are some of the rules and rituals related to your eating patterns attempts to feel less anxious and fearful, more in control? Is it hard to contemplate giving them up because they've become a part of you?

Throughout this book, you have learned a lot about yourself, including your true feelings, emotional hungers, and remarkable inner qualities. You have also discovered that much of this self-knowledge has been hidden by your disordered eating patterns and body image preoccupation. In recovery, then, you will be faced with the *certainty of change*. Thoughts and behaviors that obscure the "real you" will need to be replaced. Rules and rituals that are comfortable, but unhealthy, will need to be transformed. You'll need to take some risks by trying on different hats!

Some of your disordered eating patterns may be particularly resistant to change because they have become mixed up with your identity, which includes those characteristics that make you unique, as well as many others, such as gender, race, and group affiliations. How would friends and family describe you to someone else? What would be *your* self-description? Would you say, "I'm a bulimic" or, "I'm an anorexic" defining yourself in primarily eating-disordered terms? Or, are you ready to use more balanced, healthy self-statements, as in, "I'm a volunteer at an animal shelter. I'm funny, strong willed, and sensitive. I also have problems with food."

In this chapter let's explore your thoughts about change, identity, and new "hats." First, you'll imagine yourself as different animals that reflect your feelings about yourself now, in the past, and in the future. By describing the most appealing qualities of each, you may become clearer about which traits you'd like to develop. Then, after creating two chairs that are different—yet extraordinary in their own way—you may have some new ideas about alternative

means of securing comfort. You'll also explore what appeals to you versus what is practical and realistic, which will be especially helpful when trying to determine whether or not "trying on a new hat" might be worthwhile *for you!*

Next, you'll be inspired to take small steps forward by contemplating the notion of "change" through words and images placed within a set of footprints. Using collage materials, you will then illustrate your outer core strengths and innermost feelings, both of which influence your capability and flexibility for risk-taking when embarking on any journey. Keep these personal characteristics in mind as you design a magical hat that can aid you in making one life change and then journal about its consequences. What transformative powers would your magical hat bestow upon you to support *your* journey?

Let's shake things up a bit by trying on some different hats. Are you ready to experiment with something new?

 ## My Inner Lion and My Outer Mouse, or Visa Versa

In this task you'll address the opposite forces that reside within you using animals as metaphors. For example, a lion is a ruler who is respected and considered powerful by others in the jungle. In contrast, a mouse is tiny and often lives in fear of anything larger than itself. The roles you take on may vary from time to time, and from situation to situation.

1. Draw the animal that reflects how do you see and feel about yourself right now.

2. In the past, when perhaps you felt differently about yourself, what animal would you have been? Draw that animal.

3. If you could be any animal at all—your choice—what animal would you be? Draw that animal, too.

 **33** *Journal Entry*

What three animals did you choose for yourself? How do they differ from one another, and how are they alike? What qualities would you borrow from each animal to collectively aid you on your healing journey, and why?

Sitting in a Different Chair

A chair is a place to read a book, nestle into for contemplating ideas, rest your body, knit or crochet, talk on the phone, use the computer, eat a meal, listen to a lecture, paint a picture, play music, socialize with others, and much more. Chairs also vary in their practicality, comfort, and beauty; you may have different reactions to each chair that you sit in.

Draw an imaginary chair using colors, lines, and shapes. Think about the size, shape and materials of your chair and reflect those elements in your drawing. Now draw another chair that is unlike the first chair in every way.

34 *Journal Entry*

Look at the two chairs you just created and write about each one. Describe their differences in appearance and comfort level. What would it feel like to sit in each one, and do they support similar activities? For instance, is one better for reading or knitting, and the other better for eating a meal or socializing? In the same way that you may get accustomed to sitting in one type of chair and its specific comforts, you may be accustomed to one way of "being" and find unfamiliar things challenging. Think of a time when you had difficulty with change, and write a bit about that incident.

Stepping Out into the World

Taking risks is not easy, but each small step you take can add up to some dramatic changes. Have you ever visited a new city, especially one where the language spoken is not your native tongue? You begin by doing a bit of research, taking visual notes, gathering your confidence, and putting one foot in front of the other.

Draw your left foot and then your right foot on the page below, placing one slightly ahead of the other. Think about how you might "move forward" and make changes in your life. Using words, poetry, images, lines, and colors, fill in your left and right foot tracings with reflections about your notion of *change*.

Journal Entry

What do you notice about the feet you designed? What do they tell you about how you feel about change? Is there anything you'd like to change in your life? What might be the first step you'd need to take in order to make this change?

Your Core

These days there is much talk about "the core," though it's mostly related to physical strength and exercise. You also have a core that relates to your emotional state of being. This is where your deepest beliefs about yourself reside. In the process of making changes, you will need to spend time learning about this emotional center.

Using collage materials, find pictures and words that reflect your outer core strengths, which perhaps you allow others to see. Glue those images and words along the perimeter of the page, making sure that there are no gaps between them—like a fence. Now think about your inner core—the multifaceted beliefs and feelings you have about yourself. If you can, take a risk by finding and gluing down pictures and words that reflect these innermost (usually hidden) feelings about yourself and your world.

36 *Journal Entry*

That was surely one of the most difficult tasks in this workbook, as you were asked to let down your guard and take a big risk by disclosing some of your vulnerabilities. But in order to successfully make life changes, you *have to* look deep within. What was it like for you to do this task? How are you feeling right now? What do you notice about the words and images you used for your outer core vs. your inner core?

A New Hat

Create a hat with magical powers that would permit you to make at least one change in your life *without* feeling scared or overwhelmed. It can be colorful, black & white, tiny, outrageously crazy looking—anything! Have fun!

37 *Journal Entry*

Describe the magical powers that your new hat would have and how you'd imagine feeling when you put it on. What change would this new hat allow you to "fearlessly" make, and how do you think this change would affect your life?

CHAPTER 8

Barriers to Healing

Whether you suffer from a physical or emotional "injury," healing is an ongoing process rather than a destination. If you fall and break a bone, it takes time to mend. Similarly, emotional healing involves a progression of *curative states*. Yet healing emotional wounds is usually a more complex process. You can't simply put an ice pack on hurt feelings!

Healing emotional wounds can be challenging for many reasons. Although they are painful in their own way, emotional wounds are invisible, which makes them easy to ignore or deny. The process of healing also requires an enormous commitment of courage, faith, planning, and perseverance, not to mention time and money. Sometimes a person is not able, willing, or even ready to take on such a seemingly huge undertaking.

What's more, the prospect of facing emotional pain involves change, which, as we saw in the last chapter, has its own set of risks and rewards. Passivity or fear can then become another common barrier that keeps one "stuck" in old behaviors. It might just feel easier to go along as you always have, not only because it is familiar, but also because it might help you to avoid conflicts with other people. All of these (and more) would surely be stumbling blocks in the process of rebuilding your emotional health.

What will it take for you to face your emotional struggles, and what are the barriers that you encounter trying to do so? Do any of the following statements ring true for you?

- Letting go of familiar behaviors is scary and I may fail.
- It's easier for me to keep things "as is."
- I'm too tired to do this now.
- I'm worried that other's won't like me if I'm different than before.
- I'm angry that I'll have to "adjust" to new things.
- I feel overwhelmed and sad when I think about all that it takes to "get better."
- I may have to give up certain friends who might not be healthy for me.

Sometimes, the coping mechanisms we use to separate ourselves from the pain of emotional wounds *themselves* become barriers to healing.

Such is the case with disordered eating, which blocks out what is truly bothering you by distracting you with food and body image preoccupations. This means that one of your first challenges will be acknowledging that you have a *serious* problem. For example, ignoring the physical toll that bingeing, purging, or restricting has on your body is denying the gravity of your behaviors and preventing you from beginning the healing process.

This chapter will help you address some of the hurdles and complications that might slow down your "replenishing" journey, or even prevent you from stepping onto this path altogether.

The art and journaling experiences will explore your connections to current behaviors as well as your reluctance to modify them. A drawing of the ocean and the "environment topside" will serve as a metaphor, not only for those fears that are hidden below the surface, but also for what keeps you "anchored" in your negative behaviors. Even though they are familiar, old patterns aren't necessarily healing efforts and sometimes must be brought to the surface for examination.

Next, using abstract art and words, you'll study anxiety and anger about leaving behaviors behind, as you "drift to new places" using ocean imagery again. Freely associating to words such as "anger," "can't," "scared," and "hopeless" might further clarify some of your personal barriers and why you've positioned them in the middle of your healing pathway.

You'll also create a doormat to clarify how passivity reinforces helplessness, as you discover if anyone "steps all over you" or ignores you—and consequently squashes your potential. And last, you'll build a stonewall with rocks and pebbles that represent self-sabotaging habits.

Removing the barriers you put between yourself and the world will be rewarding and liberating. Are you ready to clear your path to healing?

Holding Your Ground

There may be numerous reasons why you're "anchored" to your disordered eating behaviors. Despite the fact that you know they are unhealthy, which is in part why you keep them a secret, you can't seem to let go of them.

Draw a line across the page that represents the surface of the ocean. Make it wavy, choppy, or calm depending on how you see your life. Add a buoy, which is a floating signal, to represent you, and connect your buoy to the ocean floor. Illustrate the weather conditions topside and the environment where the buoy is located (i.e., in the middle of the ocean versus somewhere close to land). Also include what's going on below the surface (under the water), which is typically not visible to others.

38 *Journal Entry*

What do you notice about the weather that surrounds the buoy (you)? What do you notice about the activity below the surface, which represents the secrets you keep? What are the thoughts, beliefs, feelings, and behaviors on the ocean floor to which you are "anchored" or attached?

39 *The Discomfort of Healing*

Imagine that the buoy that you just drew became detached from the ocean floor. The currents of the ocean would naturally carry it away from its original site to a new place. As the buoy floats away, what do you think will happen? Draw the next scenario in this story.

39 *Journal Entry*

Write about how it would feel to "let go" and drift to someplace new. Do you typically anticipate the best-case or worst-case scenario? How does that affect your willingness to take risks?

Uncorking the Bottle

When you don't express your authentic feelings, they float on the ocean's surface like a message wedged in a corked bottle waiting for discovery. Feelings that are "stuck" in this way can cause anger to build up, even if the original feelings were not about anger at all!

What types of anger have you experienced in the past? Circle the ones you relate to from the following list:

sad mad	frozen sad mad
anxious mad	vomiting into the toilet mad
quietly seething mad	using drugs or alcohol mad
starve it away mad	frustrated mad
act like a baby mad	raging out of control mad
scared mad	shrieking mad
get even mad	body focus mad
harming the body mad	appropriately expressed mad

…just to name a few.

Using lines, shapes, and colors, draw what your anger would look like.

40 *Journal Entry*

How did it feel to get closer to your anger? List three people or events that have left you feeling angry. What was it that evoked those feelings, and were you able to express them at the time?

Fear: Why Am I Shaking in My Boots?

Using the word "fear" as an acronym, what related words can you think of for each letter?

F ≈

E ≈

A ≈

R ≈

41 *Journal Entry*

When you think about being afraid or feeling fearful, what comes to your mind? When you think about giving up your disordered eating patterns, do you feel afraid? What is the scariest thing about leaving those behaviors behind?

Passivity: Am I Being Stepped On?

When you don't listen to and express your feelings, it's not unusual for others to see you as somewhat passive. You may not like it, but being unable to express yourself often prompts THEM to speak for YOU. At times, you may even have found yourself unable to say "no," which has allowed a few people to take advantage.

Draw a doormat that represents the ways in which you feel "stepped on." Use collage, words, colors, and shapes to illustrate these feelings.

 *Journal Entry*

What do you notice about the design (lines, shapes, and colors) of the doormat you just created? How do others disregard your feelings, take advantage of you, or ignore your needs?

Contraband? Oh, I Forgot about that Little Habit!

For our purposes, unhealthy substances and damaging behaviors are considered *contraband*, because they are barriers to recovery. This means that they allow you to avoid direct communication with your feelings by offering you "alternative" means to numb out. Diet pills, energy drinks, excessive caffeine, and laxatives are all considered contraband. So are over-exercising, hyper-sexuality, alcohol use, excessive shopping, and overspending.

Create a stone wall by drawing boulders, rocks, and pebbles of various sizes and shapes. Think about the ways you sabotage your recovery by relying on unhealthy habits to cope with feelings. Write those directly on your rock wall. Be truthful, as this is your personal workbook, and honesty will bring you closer to the health and harmony you seek.

43 *Journal Entry*

What kinds of contraband do you use and how would you feel about giving up any—or all—of it? What would help you to accomplish this very important task? Is there anyone with whom you would feel comfortable sharing this information?

CHAPTER 9

Problem Solving

Since beginning this creative journey, you've probably had a few "Aha!" moments in relation to your self-image and how you think and react. Perhaps you've recognized that a few changes are in order, such as some daily rituals that may seem comforting, yet aren't productive. Shifting how you think about yourself, your body, nutrition, relationships, and self-care takes determination. But the realization that opportunities for change exist may be just what's needed to liberate you from past patterns!

Problem solving is a way of dealing with the challenges of change by finding solutions. Sometimes just feeling overwhelmed by problems can get in the way of facing them effectively! Once "troublesome issues" have been identified, however, you can tackle them by breaking them down into more manageable parts and looking at each one systematically. This means describing what "isn't working," brainstorming other prospects, and opening yourself to creative options.

Once a problem is simplified in this way, you may be further motivated to confidently proceed in a positive direction by constructing a "game plan." This might include making a list of steps to take or asking for input and assistance from other people. You might also use the art tasks and journal exercises in this book for additional inspiration and clarity. For instance, you can:

- Literally draw the problem.

- Journal about the art you created and how you felt doing it.

- Re-look at your art from a fresh perspective by considering what *messages* your drawing or journaling might be communicating.

- Use art as a playful tool for illustrating as many solutions as you can imagine.

- Share your art with others and journal about additional solutions they are offering for the problem (move from monologue to dialogue).

- Consider all possible solutions you have identified through art and journaling, choosing one to begin your game plan!

This chapter is devoted to mapping out a route for tackling the changes you'd like to make. You'll learn about problem solving by identifying the basic steps involved in moving to a new home and then outlining a similar sequence of actions needed to discontinue one unhealthy behavior. Since support and encouragement from trusted friends and family can ease the burden of change, you will decorate and write about a laundry basket filled with "emotional wash" to create some ideas about who might help you *carry the load.*

Next, you'll draw and journal about two scenarios—what your life would be like if you let go of an unhealthy behavior as opposed to maintaining it. This will show you how a preoccupation with food and weight can interfere with your ability to problem solve by separating you from the inner guidance system of your feelings.

Finally, an illuminating feedback form will highlight potential disordered "patterns" in your life. Although this knowledge might be uncomfortable, an awareness of these patterns and their effects may *free you* to create a "staircase of healthier tools." Thinking outside the box— one mode of problem solving—often serves as a catalyst for changing the negative rituals to positive steps!

With patience, trust, and self-belief, you can initiate new ways to handle any problem. Let's figure out how to access all the inner resources and skills we know you possess!

Planning Your Move

Making changes in your life by "moving to a healthier place" is a challenge, no doubt. So the more organized, positive, and practical you are, the less overwhelmed you'll be. Imagine moving to a new home, the basic steps of which are identified below. Put each step in sequential order, and write it next to the appropriate number on the star.

- Have a goodbye party.
- Decide what you're keeping and what you're getting rid of.
- Talk about your feelings related to the move.
- Call a mover.
- Start packing.

- Announce the move to your friends/family.
- Start looking for a new home.
- Research your new location for jobs/schools/ spiritual support.
- Get boxes.
- Pick a target date for completing the move.

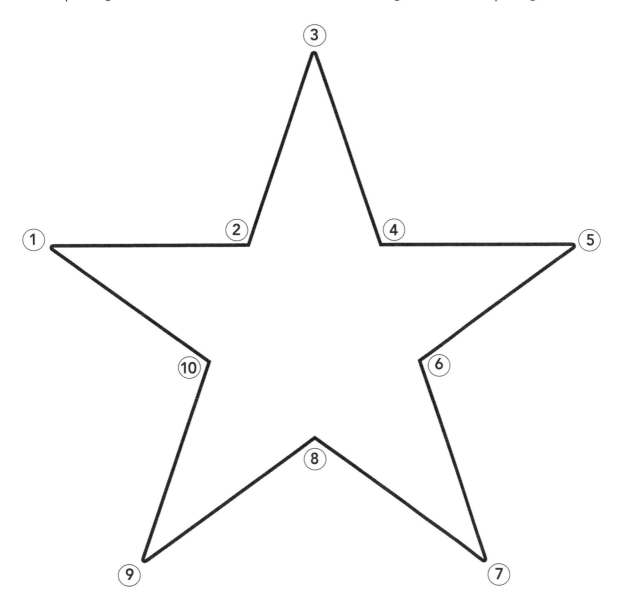

44 *Journal Entry*

Think about the sequence of steps you'd need to make to reduce or eliminate one unhealthy behavior. What behavior would you like to "leave behind," and what are the steps you anticipate needing to follow in order to succeed?

Asking for Help: The Laundry Basket

Imagine that you're taking clean clothes out of the dryer, gathering them in your arms for folding. You can't find your laundry basket, so even with your best effort some items will fall on the floor—unless you enlist others to help you carry the load.

Let's allow others to lend you a hand with your "emotional laundry" by designing a basket—with a lid—for each person you believe would be a good supporter. Decorate each one, including the person's name on the outside, and whatever you'd like them to help you with on the inside of the lid.

45 *Journal Entry*

Asking for help is difficult; however it's a requirement if you wish to fully heal. Who were your identified helpers in the laundry basket task, and why did you pick them? What did you need help with? Any surprises here?

46   *My "Precious" Disaster*

Sometimes in life we hold onto things that are not particularly helpful, like a pair of old boots that "have seen their day" or a relationship that is no longer enriching. Sometimes we even maintain possession of something at the cost of our health, giving it *precious* status. Is perhaps your obsession with your body size and what you eat precious to you, even though it leads you on a self-destructive course?

Divide the page in half and on one side draw what you believe your life would be like if you continue to devote yourself to your current "precious" behaviors. On the other side, draw what your life might be like if you devoted yourself to positive, life-affirming alternatives.

46 *Journal Entry*

What do you notice about the two drawings? How are they similar and how are they different? How do you imagine you'd *feel* if you gave up some of your "precious" unhealthy thoughts and behaviors?

Giving Yourself Feedback

Here's an opportunity for you to give yourself some honest feedback by estimating your ability to function on a multitude of levels. Below are a series of statements, each of which addresses an essential activity of daily living. Please circle the number on the rating scale below each statement that best applies to you.

I eat balanced meals daily.

1 (Never)   2 (Rarely)   3 (Sometimes)   4 (Often)   5 (Always)

I sleep 7-8 hours nightly (no more, no less).

1 (Never)   2 (Rarely)   3 (Sometimes)   4 (Often)   5 (Always)

My physical health is good, and no one has suggested that I see a medical doctor.

1 (Never)   2 (Rarely)   3 (Sometimes)   4 (Often)   5 (Always)

I spend enjoyable time with my family for at least one hour per day, unrelated to mealtime.

1 (Never)   2 (Rarely)   3 (Sometimes)   4 (Often)   5 (Always)

I have trustworthy friends whom I enjoy spending time with for at least one hour daily.

1 (Never)   2 (Rarely)   3 (Sometimes)   4 (Often)   5 (Always)

I am comfortable eating meals with others.

1 (Never)   2 (Rarely)   3 (Sometimes)   4 (Often)   5 (Always)

I am at ease going clothing shopping with others.

1 (Never)   2 (Rarely)   3 (Sometimes)   4 (Often)   5 (Always)

I can handle positive feedback from others.

1 (Never)   2 (Rarely)   3 (Sometimes)   4 (Often)   5 (Always)

I can tolerate negative feedback from others.

1 (Never)   2 (Rarely)   3 (Sometimes)   4 (Often)   5 (Always)

I exercise 3-4 days weekly and I'm at a medically safe weight.

1 (Never)   2 (Rarely)   3 (Sometimes)   4 (Often)   5 (Always)

My concentration is good and my performance (school/work) hasn't decreased.

1 (Never)   2 (Rarely)   3 (Sometimes)   4 (Often)   5 (Always)

I can stay up all day without feeling exhausted and napping.

1 (Never)   2 (Rarely)   3 (Sometimes)   4 (Often)   5 (Always)

I am not experiencing conflicts with others related to my behavior(s).

1 (Never)   2 (Rarely)   3 (Sometimes)   4 (Often)   5 (Always)

I don't feel anxious or worry about weight, body image, food, or social performance.

1 (Never)   2 (Rarely)   3 (Sometimes)   4 (Often)   5 (Always)

When I am upset, I can speak with others about it and enlist their support.

1 (Never)   2 (Rarely)   3 (Sometimes)   4 (Often)   5 (Always)

I take care of myself.

1 (Never)   2 (Rarely)   3 (Sometimes)   4 (Often)   5 (Always)

My friends and I are equally there for one another.

1 (Never) 2 (Rarely) 3 (Sometimes) 4 (Often) 5 (Always)

My mood is stable and I feel reasonably happy on a daily basis.

1 (Never) 2 (Rarely) 3 (Sometimes) 4 (Often) 5 (Always)

47 *Journal Entry*

Add up your score for each of the rating scales. Out of a possible 90 points, what do you think a "high" total would indicate? What do you think a "low" total would indicate? What is your total? Any thoughts about that?

48 *Climbing Out of the Box*

In this task, you're going to create a "staircase of tools" for mastering the discomforts of change. Begin by recalling any behaviors you have used in the past or learned from others that are helpful in the process of recovery. Then draw a set of stairs that moves upward from where you imagine yourself now. With words, collage and drawing, illustrate the various tools—one per step—in an order that would help you make steady progress out of the "box" of your old habits.

48 *Journal Entry*

What was it like to approach the discomfort of healing by first laying a foundation of tools to help you move upward? How do you think this staircase of resources will be helpful? Write about how some of these new tools you identified might useful in a current situation.

CHAPTER 10

Permission to Love Yourself

Love is a wonderful gift. Whether someone expresses love for us—or visa versa—there is no other feeling quite like it. It's truly incredible! However, when the topic of love arises, do you ever consider the love *you* have for *yourself?*

Most of us would agree that loving one's self is not a skill we were openly taught or encouraged to express. Maybe we observed situations where it was clear that someone was honoring their true selves, such as ending a toxic relationship, or rewarding themselves for a job well done. But the reverse is more often true: We learned that loving ourselves and "putting ourselves first" is self-centered and inappropriate behavior. Do any of the following beliefs about self-love ring true for you?

- Loving myself is selfish.

- I should always put other people first.

- I'm not worthy of love, even my own.

- People will only like me if I'm self-sacrificing.

- I can't say no when someone asks me to do something.

- I have a hard time accepting compliments.

The truth is that there is a big difference between loving yourself and being self-centered. A person who is self-centered is focused on their own needs before anyone else's, no matter what the situation. They are oblivious to how their actions impact others, regardless of differences in feelings and perspectives. They expect others to treat *them* as special, but do not return favor. They lack insight into their own behavior, and consequently their relationships are empty and incomplete.

In contrast, someone who is self-loving has spent time getting to know themselves at a deep level. They *work at* appreciating and liking themselves. They take the time to tune into their inner voice on a regular basis and make every effort to honor what they feel, hear, or sense without judgment. They value themselves in full, including their imperfections. They don't berate themselves for their mistakes—they learn from them.

Someone who is self-loving also knows that valuing one's self is a firm foundation for relationships with others. They have learned about compassion for others by being compassionate with themselves. They have forgiven others by forgiving themselves. They are able to be intimate with others because they trust and love who they are at the most basic level.

In this chapter, we encourage you to discover that you are worthy of experiencing yourself and your life as joyful and loving. This is not about appearances; it's about being the person you are and appreciating your place in the world. How do you get there? By listening to and honoring your inner voice, by acknowledging your unique gifts, and by attending to your needs—whether physical, spiritual, or emotional.

As you become more self-accepting, you will begin to experience yourself in a more loving way. The need to use disordered eating behaviors to hide from your feelings and lived experiences will seem far less essential. And most importantly, you will be motivated to care for your body because it is the "form" in which you get to experience love—both with others and for yourself.

The art tasks and journal exercises in this chapter will help you take some big steps towards the goal of self-love. You'll start by tuning in to your core—the home of your inner voice—and allowing a work of art (images, words, or other expression) to emerge. Next, you'll explore the various ways in which you care for yourself. How do you feed and nurture *your* heart? Do you honor and respect *all* your needs?

You'll also revisit the crystal ball that you created earlier in this workbook (p. 23). After all the hard work you've done, you will probably see that your dreams have changed and that you have new skills to make them come true. Giving yourself the gift of kindness might be one way to identify and meet your needs so that you can fulfill those dreams. What a wonderful present!

Last of all, you'll have the opportunity to convey your feelings about a variety of topics in a *free expression* project. You may choose to draw, write poetry, or journal about topics related to: food, your body, mixed feelings about giving up disordered eating patterns, the discomforts of change, guilt, self-protection, or anything else that you are feeling in the moment. This is an opportunity to find clues about your ability to appreciate and love yourself. Again, it's through openness and sincerity that self-love will rise to the surface!

So put your arms around yourself and give yourself a big hug. You're about to learn that loving yourself is not something you have to earn, but a gift you can grant yourself now—and always!

Hello, Can I Hear ME?

Take a moment to listen to your inner self. Find a spot where you can sit quietly and be alone with nothing to do and no one to worry about. Breath deeply and focus your awareness on what's taking place inside you, rather than what's going on outside. Locate the space between your heart and belly—your core—and imagine that you can hear words coming from that spot. You may have to close your eyes in order to do this, so make sure you feel psychologically safe before you start. As you stay focused on your core, use art materials to create an image on the page. It doesn't matter what you draw, or if you use words or recognizable images. As you listen in, allow your innermost expression to come forward through art making.

49 *Journal Entry*

What emotions and thoughts surfaced as you sat with yourself, listened inward, and made art? Have you ever tried to do this before? How did it feel to put your own voice above all others?

 *The Care & Feeding of the Human Heart*

Below is a list of needs that we believe are important in the caring and feeding of the human heart. They fall into specific categories such as sleep, play, work, calories for energy, relationships, and spiritual needs. Identify how you currently satisfy each of these needs. Are there any others that we neglected to include? If so, add them to the list and consider how you satisfy them.

Time I spend playing:

Things I do for fun:

Spending time with people I enjoy:

Things I do to for work or school that are intellectually stimulating:

Creative ventures I engage in:

Time devoted to resting and regaining my energy:

Time spent in healthy exercise:

Time I spend creating and eating nutritious and satisfying meals, plus one example of a nutritious meal I enjoy:

Other:

50 *Journal Entry*

How many of the statements you just filled in were easy to answer? Were there any you were unable to answer? Do you believe you adequately satisfy the physical and emotional needs of your heart? What might you change in your life in order to meet your needs more fully, more often?

 *Revisiting the Crystal Ball*

The healthier you get, the more your dreams will become attainable. Now that you've completed 50 creative tasks and journal entries about yourself, let's revisit the crystal ball from Chapter 1 (p. 23). Without looking back, draw another crystal ball and fill it in with pictures and words that illustrate your current dreams. List five of the "heart needs" (p. 131) that you'd have to develop in order to make your dreams come true.

Journal Entry

How do you feel about the hopes and dreams noted in the crystal ball you just completed? How do your current wishes compare with those depicted in your original crystal ball drawing? What do you observe about the similarities and differences between the two pictures? Now that you're able to identify what you might need, do you feel more equipped to make your dreams come true?

Free Expression

While this workbook touches on many areas of recovery through the art projects and journal entries, we're aware that some of your concerns may not have been fully explored. Below are additional issues that may affect your feeling good about yourself and living a healthy life. Draw, journal, or create poetry that expresses your thoughts and feelings about any or all of the statements below that relate to your recovery.

- Despite what others may say, I feel ambivalent about whether or not I have disordered eating patterns.

- My disordered eating and body focus is pleasurable in many ways.

- I'm not sure if my eating patterns really interfere with my life.

- I believe that my focus on food and my body protects me from other things.

- I don't know how I feel about my body.

- I don't think I can tolerate the discomforts of change.

- I don't really want to think about my body or what I feel like *in* my body.

- I feel much shame and guilt about what I'm doing to myself.

52 *Journal Entry*

What prompted you to focus on the subject(s) you did? Do your drawings and/or writings give you any clues about your ability to appreciate and love yourself?

 *A Gift of Kindness*

Giving yourself a "gift" of kind words is a gentle reminder that self-acceptance is one of the most important tools in recovery. Practicing *thought substitution* will help you replace negative, unconstructive thoughts and feelings with positive, life-affirming ones! Below, create ten absolutely encouraging, optimistic self-statements that you can pull out of your recovery toolbox on a "cloudy" day.

1.

2.

3.

4.

5.

6.

7.

8.

9.

10.

53 *Journal Entry*

What was it like to give yourself this gift of kind words? Do you think the practice of thinking positive thoughts on a daily basis could make it become more of a habit?

CHAPTER 11

Creating a New Path

Welcome to the last chapter of this workbook and the frontier of a new and soulful voyage. Cue the balloons, streamers, and music! By reaching out first with colors, lines, and shapes and then with words, you've connected with your inner voice through creativity—and a whole new pathway has been forged! You have succeeded in taking some incredibly brave steps forward! Plus, you have learned that making art and journaling are an invaluable way to strengthen your confidence and sense of self, and are therefore vital forces in guiding your healing process and recovery. Are you excited about the opportunities that lie ahead?

You've also begun to trust that having access to these new "listening-in skills" will enable you to retrieve the answers you need *whenever* you might need them. You've already devoted hours to this workbook doing art projects, writing, and facilitating internal dialogue that has resulted in a wealth of brilliant insights and inspirations from which to draw. You've been practicing powerful skills, such as:

- Discovering how to "put yourself first" as you reflect on your perceptions of your world and life

- Centering yourself by spiritually focusing inward

- Surrounding yourself with healthy, loving people who can unconditionally support you

- Learning how to use your armor safely and effectively

- Sharing feelings in order to keep your voice activated

- Acknowledging your limitations, and capitalizing on your strengths and what makes you extraordinary

- Welcoming challenges and change for a greater goal of wholeness

- Mapping out a route for tackling the changes you'd like to make

- Finding healthy resources for self-fulfillment

- Accepting and loving yourself

- Knowing when you need to seek additional help, from medical and/or therapeutic specialists, or workbooks such as this

So no matter what situation you find yourself in, you now know that creativity can clarify your true feelings and reinforce your living in harmony with the authentic YOU. And it can continue to do so for the rest of your life.

Sometimes the journey to health and wholeness means that you have to shift your perspective and create a "fresh" reality for yourself. This may entail choosing better friends, finding a less stressful job, taking risks, expressing your thoughts and feelings, or discovering new interests—all sorts of innovative opportunities! Sometimes they may seem overwhelming, and certainly life does have its challenges. But above all else, you'll be relying on your newfound ability to tune into an internal guidance system that will direct you towards recovery and healing.

We encourage you to cultivate this relationship with your inner voice by listening to and honoring its truth, and by practicing compassion towards yourself and others as you continue to make way for a fuller existence.

The creative focus of this final chapter is to review the changes you've initiated and speak honestly about your future aspirations and how you plan to reach them. You'll begin by feeding your soul with laughter and play. Having space to let loose and be silly will not only be fun, but it will also attract positive forces into your life. One of these forces is a "wise inner self," whom you will embody in a drawing or collage representation. This confident and loving side of you will dialogue with the side that is less secure and needs reassurance. You'll be surprised by what they can teach each other!

You'll also envision a path leading from your current location to a brand new one, including the weather and geography along the way. Placing yourself in the picture will show you where you see yourself and your progress on this "road" to recovery. Though you might have to navigate around some "road blocks," staying on this path is critical to reaching your final healthy destination!

Next, you'll revisit the questions you posed at the beginning of this workbook about your eating patterns, body image, feelings, and life. Now, though, you've re-established a friendship with a wise inner self, which may have given you a new perspective.

Last of all, it's time to once again don your chef's hat and bake a revised "pie of your life." Much like the one you created in the beginning of this book, the wedges of this pie will illustrate what's going on in your current daily life. You can then compare it with the earlier pie you completed on page 15. Hopefully some tasty and appetizing changes to your recipe for a healthier life will be evident!

You are at the gateway of a vibrant and wondrous world, which is welcoming you with open arms. We congratulate you on all your hard work. Believe in yourself and your ability to use art and journaling to make your dreams come true. Take one more step in that direction, as you turn the page and create the next chapter of your life!

54 A Healthy Heart Is a Playful Heart

Laughter is the best medicine and a great way to "feed" the soul. It's so important to laugh, play, have fun, and experience joy—at every age. How about creating a playroom for yourself? Make it any shape or size you want, and add a variety of details, from the wall color, rugs, furniture, staircase, windows and lighting, to the games, toys, books, and crafts. Either draw items or add small pictures.

54 *Journal Entry*

What would it be like to spend time in the playroom you just created? What needs of yours would be satisfied if you played there? List one playful activity that you'd like to try each day of the week.

 *Tapping into Your Inner Wisdom*

In this task you'll be exploring two sides of yourself. First, draw a figure that represents your wise and confident side. Perhaps collage words and images that connote wisdom and confidence onto it. Now draw another figure that represents the side of you that is less confident and needs reassurance; feel free to add collage materials, as well. If the two parts of you were to speak to one another, what would they say?

55 *Journal Entry*

What did the less confident part of you learn from the wise self? What did the confident part of you learn from the self that needs reassurance? Are you aware that you have the wisdom to answer many of your own questions by reflecting in this way?

56 The Pathway

Pathways, like tunnels, bridges, roads, and trails, connect one location to another. When you choose a new path, you leave one place and are *in process* until you reach a final destination. Draw any type of pathway that could take you from one spot to another. Include the place you're leaving and the new "home," as well as the weather and surroundings. Place yourself somewhere in the picture.

56 *Journal Entry*

What type of pathway did you create? What might the terrain and weather suggest in terms of how you're feeling about this journey? What do you notice about where you placed yourself in the picture?

 *In The Beginning*

Now, let's revisit the first entry you made in this workbook on page 13. At that time you made a list of questions you had about your eating patterns, the way you viewed your body, issues in your life, and how you felt about yourself. Copy your original list of questions below and then answer them here.

1.

2.

3.

4.

5.

6.

57 *Journal Entry*

Do you realize how much insight and clarity you've gained through your artwork and journal reflections in this workbook? Are you more comfortable managing your life now and do you feel confident that you can succeed?

 *Baking a New Pie of Your Life*

Now that you know more about yourself, it's time to bake a new "Pie of Your Life," similar to the one in Chapter 1 (p. 15). Make wedges for the different activities in your life, and don't forget to include any new ones you might have added since you started this workbook!

58 *Journal Entry*

Now compare the "Pie of Your Life" on page 15 to the one on page 149. What are some of changes you've made and insights you've gained? Journal about how this feels and about accomplishing this creative journey!

DEAR READER

Congratulations on all the creative work you have done! You now have a workbook full of insights, honesty, and inner wisdom to support your recovery. You can always reread chapters to strengthen the progress you've made, or repeat specific projects in your search for deeper understanding. In any case, we hope you'll continue to use art and journaling as tools for recovery. Remember, creativity connects us to our inner voice, and healing occurs when we listen.

We want to acknowledge you for being brave and taking the necessary risks to learn more about yourself. We hope that embracing your inner voice will empower you to continue to make healthy choices so that you will live a happy, fulfilling life.

Mindy & Maureen

ART SUPPLY RESOURCES

There are many sources for purchasing art supplies. The list below contains several Internet sites that might be helpful, and don't forget about your local art supply store! You will also find that many drug stores, grocery stores, and dollar stores sell inexpensive materials that are not professional grade but are well suited for the purposes of this workbook.

- A.C.Moore Arts & Crafts (888) 226-6673
  acmoore.com

- Crayola (800) 272-9652
  crayola.com

- Dick Blick (800) 828-4548
  dickblick.com

- Michael's Arts & Crafts (800) 642-4235
  michaels.com

- Nasco Arts & Crafts (800) 558-9595
  enasco.com

- Pearl Paint (800) 451-7327
  pearlpaint.com

- S & S Arts and Crafts (800) 288-9941
  ssww.com

- Sax Arts and Crafts (800) 558-6696
  saxarts.com

- Utrecht Art (800) 223-9132
  utrechtart.com

PROFESSIONAL ORGANIZATIONS

The organizations listed below are valuable resources for individuals with disordered eating, family members, and professionals. While this is only a partial list, each Internet site has additional links that may also be helpful for recovery.

Academy for Eating Disorders (AED)

This global, multidisciplinary, professional organization provides cutting-edge training and education, inspires new developments in eating disorders research, prevention, and clinical treatments.

>111 Deer Lake Road, Suite 100
>Deerfield, IL 60015
>(847) 498-4274
>aedweb.org

American Art Therapy Association (AATA)

AATA is an organization of professionals dedicated to the belief that the creative process is healing and life enhancing. They provide standards of professional competence and develop and promote knowledge about the field of art therapy. See the AATA website for local art therapists.

>11160-C1 South Lakes Drive, Suite 813
>Reston, VA 20191
>(888) 290-0878
>arttherapy.org

Eating Disorders Anonymous (EDA)

This is a fellowship of individuals who share their experience, strength and hope in order to solve common problems and help each other recover from their eating disorders. Meeting times and locations are available at the website.

>18233 N. 16th Way
>Phoenix, AZ 85022
>(616) 712-8000 access code 624784#
>eatingdisordersanonymous.org

Eating Disorders Coalition for Research, Policy & Action (EDC)

This group of organizations is dedicated to advancing the federal government's recognigion of eating disorders as a public health priority.

>720 7th St. NW
>Suite 300
>Washington, DC 20001
>(202) 543-9570
>eatingdisorderscoalition.org

Eating Disorder Referral and Information Center

This site provides free information and treatment referrals for all forms of eating disorders.

2923 Sandy Pointe, Suite 6
Del Mar, CA 92014-2052
(858) 481-1515
edreferral.com

Gürze Books

The publisher of this book, Gürze Books has specialized in eating disorders resources since 1980. Their comprehenisve website includes books, free articles, treatment referrals, NEDA merchandise, and much more. The *Gürze Eating Disorders Resource Catalogue* is available for free upon request.

P.O. Box 2238
Carlsbad, Ca. 92018
(800) 756-7533
bulimia.com

International Association of Eating Disorders Professionals (IAEDP)

IAEDP provides outstanding education and high-level training to an international, multidisciplinary group of healthcare treatment providers who treat the full spectrum of eating disorder problems.

PO Box 1295
Pekin, IL 61555-1295
(800) 800-8126
iaedp.com

National Association of Anorexia Nervosa and Associated Disorders (ANAD)

ANAD strives to educate the general public and professionals in the healthcare field to be more aware of eating disorders and methods of treatment. They sponsor local support groups, which can be located through the website.

Box 7
Highland Park, IL 60035
(630) 577-1330
anad.org

National Eating Disorders Association (NEDA)

NEDA is the largest U.S. nonprofit organization dedicated to expanding public understanding of eating disorders and promoting access to quality treatment. They have prevention programs, publish and distribute educational materials, have a helpline, and work to change the cultural, familial, and interpersonal factors that contribute to the development of eating disorders.

603 Stewart Street, Suite 803
Seattle, WA 98101-1264
Helpline: (800) 931-2237
(206) 382-3587
neda.org

Something Fishy

This comprehensive website is dedicated to raising awareness and providing support to people with eating disorders and their loved-ones.

(866) 690-7239
something-fishy.org

ACKNOWLEDGMENTS

We'd like to acknowledge those individuals who personally and professionally helped us reach this point in our life journey by enlightening us about the importance of imagery in the healing process. This includes our professors in the Creative Arts in Therapy program at Drexel (formerly Hahnemann) University, and our colleagues in the art therapy and eating disorder community. We are especially grateful to the professional staff at the Eating Disorders Treatment Center in Marlton, NJ, for nurturing our vision and allowing us to develop the art therapy program there.

We are equally indebted to the clients in our private practices, and at the Eating Disorders Treatment Center. Thank you for courageously sharing your creative renderings with us for the last three decades and for validating the creative tasks we included in this workbook. We could not have completed it without your help!

We'd also like to express our gratitude to Lindsey and Leigh Cohn at Gürze Books for their creative insights, enthusiasm, and brilliant collaborative editing. Your wisdom was invaluable, and we thank you for your teaching and patience. Blessings to you both!

Finally, we are indebted to the musicians whose melodies kept our writing flowing, to our belly-dancing mentors who grounded us when our imaginations were whirling, and to our family and friends for their unconditional love.

Questionnaire
The Use Of Art/Journaling In Your Recovery

We'd appreciate your input about the combined use of art and journaling in your recovery by completing this anonymous questionnaire. Your feedback is helpful to professionals, as well as others struggling with disordered eating problems.

Please email or send your responses to:

Mindy Jacobson-Levy & Maureen Foy-Tornay
505 Old York Road, Suite 100
Jenkintown, PA 19046
mindyjacobsonlevy@gmail.com

Thank you for your time.

1. Before you completed this workbook, had you ever used art or journaling for self-expression? If so, how did you use art and what materials did you work with most often? How did you use journaling?

2. If you've been in therapy before, what types of treatment did you find most helpful? What was least beneficial?

3. How did you feel when you first started using our workbook? What felt most comfortable for you? What was most challenging for you?

4. When you completed all the tasks in our workbook, did you feel more comfortable using the combined art/journaling expressive modalities? Please elaborate on this.

5. Do you believe that completing our workbook increased your awareness and insight into your disordered eating? Have you noted any changes in terms of your recovery that you might attribute to the use of this book?

ABOUT THE AUTHORS

Mindy Jacobson-Levy, MCAT, ATR-BC, LPC is a Board Certified, registered art psychotherapist and a licensed professional counselor in Pennsylvania and New Jersey. She has been in private practice since 1980 and provides individual and group art psychotherapy treatment and counseling services for adolescents and adults. Mindy has numerous publications, and clinically supervises graduate students attending Drexel University's Creative Arts in Therapy Program. She also supervises professional ATR candidates, and provides case consultations for professionals who'd like to enhance their clinical knowledge in the United States and abroad. Ms. Jacobson-Levy is a credentialed, professional member of the American Art Therapy Association, Delaware Valley Art Therapy Association, International Society for the Study of Trauma & Dissociation, and National Eating Disorders Association. In 1996 she received the Honorary Lifetime Member Award from the Delaware Valley Art Therapy Association, which is a prestigious annual award bestowed upon a professional art therapist for contributions to the field. She specializes in eating disorders, trauma/dissociation, depression, and women's issues.

Maureen Foy-Tornay, MA, ART-BC, LPC is a board certified, registered art psychotherapist, and licensed professional counselor at Philadelphia University. She has been in private practice since 2002, and is a clinical supervisor for Creative Arts in Therapy graduate students at Drexel University. Maureen utilizes visualization, art, and journaling in the treatment setting, and specializes in eating disorders, depression, and trauma. Maureen is a credentialed, professional member of the American Art Therapy Association, Delaware Valley Art Therapy Association, and National Eating Disorders Association.

Order at bulimia.com
Or by phone 800/756-7533

Finding Your Voice through Creativity is available through most booksellers or may be ordered directly from the Gürze Books website, *bulimia.com*, or by phone 800/756-7533.

FREE Catalogue

The Eating Disorders Resource Catalogue features books on eating and weight-related topics, including body image, size acceptance, self-esteem and more. It also includes listings of nonprofit associations and treatment facilities and is handed out by therapists, educators, and other health care professionals around the world.

bulimia.com

Visit our website for additional resources, including many free articles, hundreds of books, and links to organizations, treatment facilities and other websites.

eatingdisordersblogs.com

EatingDisordersBlogs.com is a website with author blogs for connecting with others about food and feelings, healthy eating, family concerns, and recovery issues.

Gürze Books has specialized in eating disorders publications and education since 1980.